The Little Book of Role Play

by Sally Featherstone
Illustrations by Martha Hardy

LITTLE BOOKS WITH **BIG** IDEAS

First published in the UK by Featherstone Education, 2001
Published 2010 by Featherstone, A&C Black
This edition published 2013 by Featherstone
An imprint of Bloomsbury Publishing Plc
50 Bedford Square, London, WC1B 3DP
www.bloomsbury.com

ISBN 978-1-9022-336-28

Text © Sally Featherstone, 2001
Illustrations © Martha Hardy, 2006
Cover photographs © Shutterstock

10 9 8 7 6 5 4 3 2 1

A CIP record for this publication is available from the British Library.

Printed in Great Britain by Latimer Trend & Company Limited.

This book is produced using paper that is made from wood grown in
managed, sustainable forests. It is natural, renewable and recyclable.
The logging and manufacturing processes conform to the environmental
regulations of the country of origin.

To see our full range of titles
visit www.bloomsbury.com

Contents

Introduction

This book is one of the titles in a series of Little Books, which explore aspects of practice within the Early Years Foundation Stage in England. The books are also suitable for practitioners working with the early years curriculum in Wales, Northern Ireland and Scotland, and in any early years setting catering for young children.

Across the series you will find titles appropriate to each aspect of the curriculum for children from two to five years, giving practitioners a wealth of ideas for engaging activities, interesting resources and stimulating environments to enrich their work across the Early Years Curriculum.

Each title also has information linking the activity pages to the statutory Early Years curriculum for England. This title has been updated to include the revised Early Learning Goals published by the Department for Education in March 2012. The full set of 17 goals is included in the introduction to each book, and the activity pages will refer you to the relevant statements to which each activity contributes.

For the purposes of observation and assessment of the children's work in each activity, we recommend that practitioners should use each of the 'revised statements' as a whole, resisting any impulse to separate the elements of each one into short phrases.

The key goals for this title are highlighted, **although other goals may be included on some pages.**

PRIME AREAS

Communication and language

① **Listening and attention:** children listen attentively in a range of situations. They listen to stories, accurately anticipating key events and respond to what they hear with relevant comments, questions or actions. They give their attention to what others say and respond appropriately, while engaged in another activity.

② **Understanding:** children follow instructions involving several ideas or actions. They answer 'how' and 'why' questions about their experiences and in response to stories or events.

③ **Speaking:** children express themselves effectively, showing awareness of listeners' needs. They use past, present and future forms accurately when talking about events that have happened or are to happen in the future. They develop their own narratives and explanations by connecting ideas or events.

Physical development

① **Moving and handling:** children show good control and co-ordination in large and small movements. They move confidently in a range of ways, safely negotiating space. They handle equipment and tools effectively, including pencils for writing.

② **Health and self-care:** children know the importance for good health of physical exercise, and a healthy diet, and talk about ways to keep healthy and safe. They manage their own basic hygiene and personal needs successfully, including dressing and going to the toilet independently.

Personal, social and emotional development

① **Self-confidence and self-awareness:** children are confident to try new activities, and say why they like some activities more than others. They are confident to speak in a familiar group, will talk about their ideas, and will choose the resources they need for their chosen activities. They say when they do or don't need help.

② **Managing feelings and behaviour:** children talk about how they and others show feelings, talk about their own and others' behaviour, and its consequences, and know that some behaviour is unacceptable. They work as part of a group or class, and understand and follow the rules. They adjust their behaviour to different situations, and take changes of routine in their stride.

③ **Making relationships:** children play co-operatively, taking turns with others. They take account of one another's ideas about how to organise their activity. They show sensitivity to others' needs and feelings, and form positive relationships with adults and other children.

SPECIFIC AREAS

Literacy

① Reading: children read and understand simple sentences. They use phonic knowledge to decode regular words and read them aloud accurately. They also read some common irregular words. They demonstrate understanding when talking with others about what they have read.

② Writing: children use their phonic knowledge to write words in ways which match their spoken sounds. They also write some irregular common words. They write simple sentences which can be read by themselves and others. Some words are spelt correctly and others are phonetically plausible.

Mathematics

① Numbers: children count reliably with numbers from 1 to 20, place them in order and say which number is one more or one less than a given number. Using quantities and objects, they add and subtract two single-digit numbers and count on or back to find the answer. They solve problems, including doubling, halving and sharing.

② Shape, space and measures: children use everyday language to talk about size, weight, capacity, position, distance, time and money to compare quantities and objects and to solve problems. They recognise, create and describe patterns. They explore characteristics of everyday objects and shapes and use mathematical language to describe them.

Understanding the world

① People and communities: children talk about past and present events in their own lives and in the lives of family members. They know that other children don't always enjoy the same things, and are sensitive to this. They know about similarities and differences between themselves and others, and among families, communities and traditions.

② The world: children know about similarities and differences in relation to places, objects, materials and living things. They talk about the features of their own immediate environment and how environments might vary from one another. They make observations of animals and plants and explain why some things occur, and talk about changes.

③ **Technology:** children recognise that a range of technology is used in places such as homes and schools. They select and use technology for particular purposes.

Expressive arts and design

① **Exploring and using media and materials:** children sing songs, make music and dance, and experiment with ways of changing them. They safely use and explore a variety of materials, tools and techniques, experimenting with colour, design, texture, form and function.

② **Being imaginative:** children use what they have learnt about media and materials in original ways, thinking about uses and purposes. They represent their own ideas, thoughts and feelings through design and technology, art, music, dance, role-play and stories.

How to use this book

Role play is a vital part of children's education – in the Early Years Foundation Stage and beyond. It forms the basis for storytelling, writing and social development. Role play gives opportunities for children to play out the events they observe and experience. It provides experience of real life situations in which they can practise their problem solving and communication skills. Role play develops children's creativity and, above all, it is fun!

There are three major types of role play:

▶ domestic play – where the home and family are at the centre, with food to prepare and jobs to do etc.

▶ transactional play – where goods and services are exchanged for money, shops, travel agents, vets, etc.

▶ imagined worlds – those places where stories dwell, or places the children are unlikely to visit, such as the moon or under the sea.

In settings where more than one of these types are offered, the play which develops is deeper, more complex and more intense, giving richer experiences for children.

All three types of play can be provided through 'whole body' play with dressing up and life-sized equipment; through 'small world' play such as Lego, Playmobil, etc; and through the use of puppets.

On each of the pages in this book you will find:

▶ Three linked situations for role play, one from each of the above types.

▶ Suggested resources and equipment

▶ Key vocabulary

▶ Writing and numeracy links and opportunities

Children will also relish being involved in the preparation of new role play areas. Their ideas, suggestions and adaptations will enhance the activities, so give them ownership and let them help!

When you have used the ideas in the threes, as they are presented on each page, you could cut the pages along the dotted lines to make a whole new range of variations!

Resources

male and female clothing

cooking utensils, including those from other cultures and countries

a baby doll and baby clothes

shopping baskets and bags

money (real if possible)

plastic food, colour coded place settings

blankets and pillows

TV/washer/drier/iron

books and magazines

phone and directory

Vocabulary

family members

meals and times

food names

cooking

clothing

Literacy links

shopping lists

phone numbers

messages

forms

letters

Maths links

place settings

house numbers

money

measuring (eg. for new curtains)

Resources

shop counter (a table)

a till

money (preferably real)

purses

cans, packets, boxes plastic bottles

dough plastic fruit and vegetables

apron/overall for shopkeeper

shopping bags

open/closed notice

shopping trolley

Vocabulary

bag

list

money

pay

door

open

closed

want

please

thank you

Good morning

Literacy links

prices

labels

notices

Maths links

money

shape

counting

time

Resources

sand or soil

diggers

dumpers

houses

signs or road mat

houses

cars and lorries

diggers

road signs

traffic lights

workmen (play people)

guttering and drainpipes

Vocabulary

dig

move

carry

lift

under

over

behind

in front

beneath

workman

Literacy links

signs and notices

clipboards

Maths links

shapes

position

direction

time

House

Domestic

A detached or semi-detached house, a flat or bungalow.

Or try a terrace (2 or 3 houses next door to each other).

Corner shop

Transactional

A simple table or bench will do. Why not try an outdoor shop, supermarket, street market or stall?

You could even have a summer fair.

Under the ground
(in a sand tray)

Imagined places

Digging, road mending, house building and exploring all provide situations underground.

Try some plastic guttering to make roads and drainpipe for tunnels.

Resources
doll's or other house
bears
small world doll
chairs
beds
bowls
spoons
green felt or fake grass
for outside
lego or other trees for the
wood

Vocabulary
big, middle size, small
mother, father, baby
next, before, after
broken
mend
sad, upset
scared

Literacy links
notices
sequencing events
letters and notes

Maths links
size
one to one matching

- -

Resources
tables and chairs
crockery and cutlery,
teapots, honey jars
bowls for porridge
trays, menus
apron for waiter
notebook for orders
chef's hat, pans etc for
cook
signs and notices
open and closed signs
price lists
plastic flowers for tables

Vocabulary
please/thank you
order
choose
bring/fetch/take
how many?
what would you like?
wait
porridge
honey
table
menu
spoon
next

Literacy links
prices
menus
notices
orders

Maths links
money
shape
counting

- -

Resources
trees and creepers made of
paper, hanging from ceiling
trees on stands or posts
plants and flowers (real
or made)
animals (soft toys)
a winding path (carpet off
cuts)
compass
torch
bag or blanket
map

Vocabulary
scary
brave
creepy
hiding
winding
shelter
leaves
twigs
branches
tree trunk
wind/rain
dark
lost

Literacy links
direction signs
maps and plans
finding your way
what's in a wood?
feeling frightened/lost

Maths links
direction
size

The Three Bears' House
(small world)

Domestic

A doll's house, a Playmobil house or two boxes stuck on top of each other can make a house for this activity.

Thatch it with straw for a realistic look.

The Three Bears' Café

Transactional

The menu in this café might contain only foods mentioned in the story, or the foods bears like!

Honey sandwiches, porridge, honey cakes – all in small, medium and large portions.

The Three Bears' wood

Imagined places

This wood could be indoors or out.

It could be creepy or safe, light or very dark!

Hang trees from lines or stand in buckets or blocks, indoors or out.

Make paths and streams on the floor.

Resources

male and female clothing
baby animals
shopping baskets/bags
money (real if possible)
plastic food and colour
coded place settings
blankets and pillows
vet's bag and coat
books and magazines
phone and directory
diary/appointment book
calendar
prescription forms

Vocabulary

family members
meals and times
food names
cooking
look after
better/worse
animal names
medicines and
treatments

Literacy links

shopping lists
phone numbers
messages
forms
letters

Maths links

place settings
house numbers
money
time
size

Resources

overall for vet
vet's bag with a
thermometer and other
vet's instruments
chairs in waiting room
soft toy pets
carry-boxes to take animals
to the vet
magazines in waiting room
table for examining
receptionist's desk
scales
leaflets and notices

Vocabulary

names of different
kinds of pets
waiting
medicine
weigh
feed
drink
take turns
number
thermometer
injection

Literacy links

files and notes
prescriptions
posters on caring for pets
opening times
magazines and non-fiction
books

Maths links

weighing
money
ordinal numbers for waiting
room

Resources

sand, playmat or play tray
space monsters, imaginary
animals
small world people
cages or fences
money
carrying boxes

Vocabulary

cost/price/pay/change
too big/fierce, etc.
frightening
feed
what will it need to
drink? eat?
where will it sleep?
how will we get it
home?
where will we take it
for a walk?

Literacy links

labels
prices

Maths links

counting
sorting
size/shape/colour

Vet's house

Domestic

A vet's house might have animal magazines and books, and maybe an animal to look after.

The vet will need a phone and a diary or appintment book, and of course, a vet's coat and bag.

Vet

Transactional

How do vets look after animals?

What do they do to cure sick animals?

What else do vets do?

Fantasy pet shop

Imagined places

What if your pet was a dinosaur?

Or a space monster?

Set up a fantasy pet shop. Who do you think the customers might be?

Resources

male and female clothing
cooking utensils, including those from other cultures and countries
baby doll and baby clothes
shopping baskets and bags
money (real if possible)
plastic food and colour coded place settings
blankets and pillows
TV
books and magazines
phone and directory

Vocabulary

domestic vocabulary plus the work vocabulary of a zoo
late
overtime
animal names
new animals
sick animals
babies
animal food
cleaning cages

Literacy links

messages
books and magazines
notes and lists

Maths links

time
size and shape

Resources

zoo animals
cages
floor or table mat
fences or cages
tickets for entry

Vocabulary

animal names
new animals
sick animals
babies
animal food
cleaning cages
better
worse

Literacy links

cage labels
opening times
food lists

Maths links

sorting
counting

Resources

jeep made from boxes or chairs
steering wheel
cameras and notebooks
maps
jungle hats
camouflage shirts
books about animals
backcloth of jungle or safari country

Vocabulary

drive
dangerous
photos
video
keep still
hide
run away
camouflage
names of jungle animals

Literacy links

clipboards
pictures and books of jungle animals
maps

Maths links

shapes
position
counting

Zoo keeper's cottage

Domestic

Link the domestic play to small world to reinforce language, make connections and extend concepts.

Zoo (small world)

Transactional

Make a zoo for the zoo keeper.

Sort the animals, feed them, arrange for visitors to come and see them.

Jungle safari

Imagined places

A trip to the jungle to photograph wild animals and watch them from the safety of a jeep.

You need cameras and notebooks for the safari. Some of the children could dress up as jungle animals!

Resources

male and female clothing
cooking utensils, including
those from other cultures
and countries
baby doll and baby clothes
shopping baskets and bags
money (real if possible)
plastic food and colour
coded place settings
blankets and pillows
TV
books and magazines
phone and directory

Vocabulary

domestic vocabulary
take away
hungry
fetch
order
wrap
hot
big or small
pay/cost
money
bag

Literacy links

lists
writing orders
making signs and notices

Maths links

money
counting

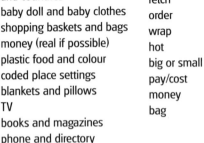

Resources

foam chips
fish from dough or clay
sausages
burgers
mushy peas
ketchup/vinegar bottles
salt shakers
paper to wrap chips
polystyrene pots for
peas
money and a till
signs and lists
bags

Vocabulary

what would you like?
how many?
large or small portion?
take away
salt and vinegar?
wrapped or open?
next please

Literacy links

price lists
note pads
posters
menus

Maths links

size
quantity
money

Resources

a water tray or waterway
or a magnetic fishing game
different sized fish to float
and catch
fishing boats or fishing rods
trays or boxes (to collect
the fish)

Vocabulary

catch
fish
big/small
collect
count
weigh
sell

Literacy links

fish and underwater books
where food comes from
labels

Maths links

numbers (for fishing game)
size

House

Domestic

Real life domestic play.

A family setting to send out from for a take away!

Ring the changes by making take away menus for different sorts of food – pizzas, curry, fish and chips etc.

Fish and chip shop

Transactional

A fish and chip shop complete with vinegar bottles, paper wrappings, sausages and foam chips!

(See dough recipes on page 52).

Gone fishing

Imagined places

Fishing for the fish for the chip shop.

This is a good way to begin exploring where food comes from.

You could make a fishing boat outside, and paint some sea on the ground.

You could also use a plastic aquarium to make an underwater world.

Resources

house (made or bought – lego, Playmobil or boxes)
furniture
small world people
trees and flowers for the garden
car or other vehicle big enough for the people

Vocabulary

domestic vocabulary
You could link this to the hospital or doctor by having small world ambulance, doctor, nurse, etc.

Literacy links

signs, labels, notices, street signs
books about houses

Maths links

counting

Resources

doctor's coat
doctor's bag with instruments
thermometer
plasters and ointment
pad for prescriptions
mobile phone
bleeper
dolls or other children to treat
chairs for waiting room
receptionist's desk
chair, phone, notes, etc.

Vocabulary

medicine
infectious
prescription
tablets
thermometer
temperature
rest
injection
vaccination
bandages
dressing

Literacy links

prescriptions
messages
phone book
notebook

Maths links

phone numbers

Resources

ambulance made from boxes or chairs
steering wheel
uniforms for nurses, doctors, ambulance staff
beds
medicines and equipment
bandages and plasters
chairs for visitors
flowers
bleepers and phones

Vocabulary

emergency
broken
accident
visitor
nurse
doctor
better
treatment
operation
injection
stitches
plaster
trolley
x-ray

Literacy links

clipboards
get well cards
prescriptions
name tags
books about being in hospital

Maths links

counting

Doll's house

Domestic

A doll's house can be bought, made or adapted.

Shoe boxes piled on their sides can make a block of flats or a multi-storey house.

Doctor

Transactional

A doctor's surgery is always fascinating for children.

A simple doctor's kit and a desk for the receptionist will give opportunities to play out fears and worries.

Hospital

Imagined places

A hospital stay is an imagined fear for many children.

Help them to talk about it and play out what might happen.

Resources

male and female clothing
cooking utensils
money (real if possible)
plastic food
shampoo bottles
hairspray (empty!)
hairdrier
mirrors
brushes and combs
hairclips, ribbons, beads
and bands
hair style magazines
phone and directory

Vocabulary

domestic vocabulary,
plus the work
vocabulary of
hairdressing
special occasions
wedding/birthday
party
cut and dry/trim/style
long/short
back/front/sides
straight/curly
hair extensions
plaits/fringe
weaving

Literacy links

appointments
books about special
occasions
magazines
notes and lists
cultural features of hair
and beauty

Maths links

time
length

Resources

rollers, clips and pins
shampoo and conditioner
combs
brushes
hairdriers
bottles and jars
mirrors
basins and bowls
style books
overalls
chairs
receptionist's desk
telephone/book/pen

Vocabulary

style
next please
please wait
wash and shampoo
cover
wet/(blow) dry
rollers
comb
rinse
fringe
back/front
long/short
pay

Literacy links

appointment book
labels
notices
open/closed
style books (or cut and
stick from magazines, or
use photos of the children)

Maths links

money
length
time

Resources

materials to make wigs
– paper, wool, card,
magazine pictures
a work bench or
production line
overalls/aprons
plastic cups for tea breaks
showroom or catalogue
of products
scissors, glue, etc.
polystyrene heads from
shop displays

Vocabulary

make
choose
together
work
body and face parts
colour
measure
fit
try on
curly
straight
long/short

Literacy links

notices
catalogues
prices and lists
books about factories
hair magazines

Maths links

order
shape
size
money

House

Domestic

Link the domestic play to the hairdresser to reinforce language, make connections and extend concepts. It also gets them out of the house!

Hairdresser

Transactional

'Wash', comb and style hair.

Even do nails and make-up!

Wig factory

Imagined places

Make a wig for yourself or someone else.

This provides great opportunities to talk about cultures, similarities and differences, and the world of work.

Resources
small world people

a mat or some fake grass, plastic or green paper

bikes (Lego/Playmobil)

flowers and trees

swings, slides, roundabouts, paths and flower beds

seats or benches

model swings and slides (children could make their own)

Vocabulary
play
ride
slide
push
round
path, gate
seat
pond
safe
football
game
boat
ice cream

Literacy links
notices
labels
stories and non fiction books about different parks
park rules noticeboards

Maths links
time
shape
direction

Resources
plants and plant pots
garden tools
gardening books
compost/gravel
plants
seed packets
fertilisers and plant food
overalls/aprons
till and money
watering cans
seed trays
phone
sand tray and trucks

Vocabulary
plant
grow
seed
water
sell
leaves
cost
label
look after

Literacy links
labels
price lists
growing instructions
books and magazines about gardens and plants
make a catalogue

Maths links
counting
money
weight

Resources
suspend a sheet of clear plastic between two tables for the pond

insects and other pond creatures

magnifying glasses

plastic frogs, worms and other minibeasts – or let the children make their own models

Vocabulary
under
water
wet
looks
light
mud
sleep
swim
fish
insect
frog
wiggle/fly/jump

Literacy links
reference books about minibeasts
life stories of frogs, etc.

Maths links
shape
size
position

Park (small world)

Domestic

Link the domestic play to small world to reinforce language, make connections and extend concepts.

Garden centre

Transactional

Help the children to set up a garden centre.

Link this to work on plants, minibeasts and growth.

You could also have a café or a shop with books, cakes and pots of jam.

In a pond

Imagined places

Suspend a sheet of clear plastic between two tables or units. Cover the floor underneath with brown material (edge it with fake grass).

Hang some insects over the pond, stick some to the surface and hang some fish underneath.

Crawl inside and look up!

Resources

road mat
cars
lorries
houses
people
trees
signs
traffic lights
garage

Vocabulary

park
drive
pay
ticket
left/right
stop/go
up/down
wait
shopping
town

Literacy links

notices
signs
non fiction and fiction
books
maps and plans

Maths links

counting
sorting

Resources

wheeled toys
buckets
water
washing up liquid
brushes
sponges
overalls
wellies
signs and directions
till and money
tickets

Vocabulary

wash
shampoo
ticket
wait
brush
inside/outside
shine
polish
wheels
queue
turn

Literacy links

signs
notices
appointments
tickets and tokens

Maths links

sorting
counting
money
capacity

Resources

fire engine
fire station
plastic tube for hoses
firemen's hats
a bell or siren
telephones

Vocabulary

drive
careful
emergency
ladder
rescue
water
hose
flames
carry
uniform
telephone
999

Literacy links

maps and plans
directions
messages

Maths links

direction

Road mat and garage (small world)

Domestic

Link the domestic play to small world by providing houses and people, not just cars.

This will reinforce language, make connections and extend concepts.

Garage and car wash (small world)

Transactional

A car wash really needs to be outside.

It is great fun for water play and for examining the parts of the wheeled toys.

Fire station

Imagined places

The fire station could be indoors or outside.

Make sure the crew take their engine to the car wash to keep it bright and clean!

Resources

tent or other covered space
sleeping bags
plastic cookware and crockery
buckets or water carriers
torches
walking sticks
maps
rucksack
sunglasses
a fake campfire or camping stove

Vocabulary

night
sleep
cook
sleeping bag
tent
outside
cold
holiday
dark
water
food
shops

Literacy links

camping stories
books and magazines
lists
instructions (eg. for putting up a tent)

Maths links

time
size and shape

Resources

tent and camping catalogues
sleeping bags
rucksacks
compass
raincoats
hats
water bottles
maps
guide books
postcards
stamps

Vocabulary

buy
size
pay
rain
fit
water
cover
wrap
bag
carry
next

Literacy links

maps
directions
instructions (eg. for putting up a tent)
lists

Maths links

direction
money

Resources

sand/water tray or cement mixing tray
small world people
sand and water
deck chairs
ice cream van
boats
sunshades and umbrellas

Vocabulary

holiday
sunshine
sunburn
swim
picnic
boat
ride
sand
fish

Literacy links

labels and notices

Maths links

size
shape

Tent

Domestic

Pop-up tents or other shelters provide a different venue for domestic play. If you haven't got one, tie a rope between two trees or posts and drape a blanket over it.

Camping shop

Transactional

Visit the camping shop to get the things you need for your trip.

The beach
(small world in the sand/water tray)

Imagined places

Give the children the materials to make a beach, then use the small world people to make stories and situations.

Resources

towels
dressing gowns
shampoo, etc. bottles
tray with tea things
trolley for 'room service'
magazines and travel guides
hotel guides
bags and suitcases
telephone
booking forms
signing-in book

Vocabulary

trip
visit
booking
stay
reservation
nights
breakfast
room service
restaurant
taxi
luggage
shop

Literacy links

forms
letters
postcards
bookings
diaries and calendars
tickets
holiday stories

Maths links

dates
times
directions
room numbers

Resources

forms
brochures
tickets
phone
computer
posters
desk for travel agent
notice board for special offers
foreign money
cheques
travel books

Vocabulary

book
aeroplane
ticket
money
hotel
fly
rain
boat
ferry
pay
sunny
skiing
holiday

Literacy links

letters
forms
days and months
labels for luggage
names and addresses
books about foreign places
holiday stories

Maths links

time
distance
money

Resources

airport floor mat (or make your own on a sheet of plastic; use markers or paint mixed with pva)
planes
lorries
coaches
cars

Vocabulary

fly
land
board
direction
travel
wait
queue
luggage carousel
check in

Literacy links

direction
stories about flying
maps and plans

Maths links

counting
time

Hotel room

Domestic

Link the domestic play to other home situations to reinforce language, make connections and extend concepts.

Travel agent

Transactional

Book a holiday or a stay in the hotel.

There are lots of opportunities here to write, fill in forms, change money and find out about the world.

Airport
(small world)

Imagined places

A small world airport will give further opportunities to explore unfamiliar or rarely experienced situations.

Don't forget a car park with cars and some small people.

Resources

home situation items such as plates, cups and cutlery
dishwasher
phone and phone book
fast food leaflets
money (real if possible)

Vocabulary

send
phone
choose
topping
cheese, tomato, mushroom
pay
bring
ask
number
small
medium
large

Literacy links

domestic stories
fact books about food
recipes

Maths links

size
shape
money

Resources

table for cooking dough or sponge for pizzas 'toppings'
rolling pins and boards
money (real if possible)
pizza boxes
bike with trailer or basket to take pizzas
aprons and chef's hats for bakers

Vocabulary

small
medium
large
topping
food words
cook
roll
thick
thin
cheese

Literacy links

price lists
menus
recipes
leaflets

Maths links

prices
size
money

Resources

play mat (or make your own)
cars
houses and shops
road signs
diggers and dumpers
traffic lights
workmen

Vocabulary

dig
hole
fill
traffic
under
sand, cement, tarmac
no through road
no entry
stop/go
queue

Literacy links

fiction and non fiction about roads, diggers, holes, etc.
signs
directions

Maths links

direction
size

House

Domestic

Link the domestic play to other home situations to reinforce language, make connections and extend concepts.

Take away pizzas

Transactional

Take away meals are very familiar to most children.

Use dough or sponge to make the pizzas, then paint the fillings. Or set up a table to make their own to order.

How about making some real pizzas!

Road works
(small world)

Imagined places

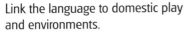

Road works are available in Lego, Playmobil and other sets.

Link the language to domestic play and environments.

You could also set up a full size road works outside, complete with signs, diversions and holes.

Resources

home situation items such
as plates, cups, cutlery,
dishwasher
phone and phone book
photo albums
smart dressing up
clothes, hats
camera
veils (curtain nets)
fake flower bouquets
diaries and calendars
phone books
wedding magazines

Vocabulary

invite
wedding
marry
best man
bride, groom
mother in law
father in law
reception
food
wedding cake
relations
bridesmaid
page

Literacy links

invitations
cards
labels
lists of guests, etc.
menus
photo album

Maths links

calendars
diaries
time
money

Resources

fake jewels, foils, card
foam for cakes
cake decorations
cake boxes
order book
hats
fake flowers
telephone
cheap rings and
bracelets
gifts and gift boxes
wrapping paper
ribbon, labels, cards

Vocabulary

cost
size
measure
time
pay
choose
jewel
gold/silver
gift

Literacy links

lists
labels
catalogues
labels
cards

Maths links

measuring
money

Resources

puppets (or make your
own wedding characters)
screen on a table or
puppet theatre
objects for puppets to use
posters
chairs for the audience
tickets and chair
numbers

Vocabulary

play
puppeteer
hand
work
watch
show
character
story
(also wedding
vocabulary from
above situations)

Literacy links

posters
labels
signs

Maths links

tickets and prices
(money)
ordinal numbers on chairs

Wedding

Domestic

A familiar setting for the preparation of a special event!

Go to the wedding shop for the things you need.

Don't forget to take some photos!

Wedding shop

Transactional

Rings, cakes, clothes, gifts – all available from the Wedding Shop!

Come and choose from our catalogue!

Puppet show

Imagined places

Puppets extend children's language and have a different dimension of play.

You could have the characters from a wedding or familiar story.

A clothes airer or a big box will make a theatre.

Resources

usual house equipment
plus:
baby bath
nappies
pram
cot
baby clothes
bottles and dummies
baby toys
(try twin babies for a
change!)

Vocabulary

baby
cry
feed
change
smile
doctor, health visitor
teething
lullaby
sleep
awake
play
bath
nappy

Literacy links

baby cards
lullabies
stories about babies
baby talk
shopping lists

Maths links

time
weight
capacity (feeds)

Resources

shop counter or table
cash register
plastic or real money
bags and carriers
baby clothes and items
empty bottles for tablets
or medicines
labels
notices
chairs to wait on
chemist's white coat
pens
scales

Vocabulary

buy
list
need
prescription
doctor
medicine
wait
nappies
packet
sick
weigh

Literacy links

prescriptions
shopping lists
stories
posters

Maths links

weight
time (open/closed)
money

Resources

posters and leaflets
scales
nurse's uniform
doctor's white jacket
'injections'
pens and paper
lists
check up cards
weight charts
length/height measures
cups of tea
pushchairs

Vocabulary

grow/grown
heavy
long
wait
doctor
health visitor
injection
cry
warm
undress
scales
write

Literacy links

lists
records
sequences of growth
stories about babies
going out

Maths links

weight
length

House with a baby

Domestic

Babies make a good focus for domestic play – most children know (or think they know) what babies do and how to look after them.

Try twins for double the fun!

Chemist
(with baby things)

Transactional

Take the baby to the chemist for baby food, bottles or teething medicine.

Some chemists sell clothes, rattles, teething rings and other baby things.

Baby clinic
(outside)

Imagined places

Take a trip to the clinic to have your baby weighed and measured.

Talk to the nurse or doctor about their problems and meet other mums and dads.

Ask a health visitor or new baby to visit school.

Resources

usual house equipment
plus old fashioned items
like shopping baskets, flat
iron, aprons and caps

a dog or cat

an old fashioned range

Mother Hubbard's Cupboard

Red Riding Hood's

Grandmother's bed

3 Bears things

story book clothes

Vocabulary

Once upon a time
lived
cottage
forest
country
lane
fields
shopping
walk
garden
cooking

Literacy links

read and write stories
about cottages and the
people who live in them
fairy tales
lists
labels

Maths links

counting (eg. 3 bears)

Resources

shoes of different sizes,
several pairs the same
labels
shoe boxes
till and money
badges or uniforms for
shop assistants
rulers and foot sizers
polishes
laces
carrier bags
mirrors
notices and adverts

Vocabulary

buy
try
measure
cost
pair
fetch
like
choose
colour
shiny
buckle/laces/velcro
fasten/tie
fit/too big/too small

Literacy links

make a shoe catalogue
labels
notices
play "whose shoes are
these?" with pictures
from catalogues

Maths links

measures
money
counting in 2's

Resources

big versions of everything!
big plates
serving spoons
big tables and chairs
giant's dressing up
clothes
big books, pens, etc.
big money and a big purse
for shopping

Vocabulary

big
giant
enormous
gigantic
vast
high
huge
massive

Literacy links

giant stories
giant poems, lists, labels
different voices

Maths links

size

Grandmother's house

Domestic

A cottage makes a change of venue for domestic play. A story book character could live here.

You could thatch a sloping roof with straw or paint flowers on the outside.

Shoe shop

Transactional

A shoe shop with a wide range of sizes, even big enough for a giant, or find seven pairs of tiny shoes for the seven dwarfs.

Giant's castle

Imagined places

The giant lives in a very big house, outside the classroom or nursery or under the climbing frame.

He needs very big furniture, cutlery and clothes, he might even need new shoes or clothes for a wedding.

Resources

a different set of house things for each house, by colour, pattern, shape
different colour doors
letter box in each door
numbers on front doors
a different sort of baby for each
different occupations for each family
paper and envelopes
a phone in each

Vocabulary

next door
neighbour
visit
friends
play
garden
fence
street
different

Literacy links

stories about neighbours and friends
letters and cards
lists

Maths links

odd and even
counting

Resources

uniforms and bags
post boxes (two if you link with the homes)
letters and parcels to sort
sacks for letters
stamps
scales
a trike with a trailer
pens, paper
till and money
forms
date and franking
stamps and pads

Vocabulary

send/deliver
collect
post box
time
sort
stamp
stick
wrap
parcel
letter
form
date
van

Literacy links

stories about postmen and letters
writing letters
making parcels
addresses (make a class address book)

Maths links

money
time
weight

Resources

A cold looking grotto or igloo (polystyrene or white sheets on a frame)
post box (from a big cardboard tube)
toys and a workbench
santa and elf suits
paper for parcels
clipboards and pens
lists on the walls
reindeer and food
a sleigh made from a ride-on toy

Vocabulary

send
list/write
want
make
present
gift
hurry
in time
boy/girl
stocking
sack
sleigh/reindeer
night/chimney

Literacy links

Christmas and Santa stories and songs
poems
writing letters
lists
labels and addresses

Maths links

weight
counting

More than one house

Domestic

Several small houses can revive the idea of domestic play by providing neighbours and somewhere to visit or phone.

Post office

Transactional

A post office and postperson offer so many experiences in so many areas.

A terrace of houses makes the job much more interesting!

Santa's grotto

Imagined places

Write a letter to Father Christmas.

Post it at the Post Office and the postman will deliver it to the North Pole.

Resources

black out the windows with black paper painted with stars

usual house equipment, plus working lamps and lights, TV and TV magazines, radio, beds and bedclothes

PJs, nightdresses, slippers, dressing gowns for dressing up

phone

Vocabulary

night
dark
bedtime
watch
supper
food
late/early
pyjamas/nightie/
dressing gown
brush teeth
drink
snack

Literacy links

stories about bedtime and night

books about night time creatures

a scrap book of magazine and other night pictures

dreams and nightmares

Maths links

time

Resources

tables, table cloths, chairs and high chair

crockery, table napkins

food made from dough or sponge

trays

aprons or overalls for waiters/waitresses

order pads and pens

phone and appointment book

coat rack

menus

Vocabulary

booking
choose
like
bring
drink/eat
pudding/sweet
table
chair
order
bill
pay
please/thank you

Literacy links

stories about food and eating

menus

forms

Maths links

money
time

Resources

make a dark place with fabric or plastic

cover the floor with dark mats or plastic sheet

torches

bats

spiders and cobwebs

a tape of dripping water

a mirror

dark clothes to dress-up in will emphasise the darkness

Vocabulary

dark
scary
spooky
hang
shadow
wall
feel
webs

Literacy links

spooky stories

stories about the dark

being scared

light and dark

Maths links

shape

A house at night

Domestic

Domestic play will change at night with TV, evening meals and coming home from school and work.

You could provide a working light switch and a TV to watch.

A restaurant

Transactional

Don't stay at home, go out for a meal at the restaurant!

You could make a Curry House, an Italian, a fish and chip restaurant or a Burger Bar.

Phone first to book a table.

A cave

Imagined places

A cave is easily made in the darkest corner of your room.

Use torches to illuminate the inside and hang bats and cobwebs for a really scary experience.

A mirror is an interesting addition!

Resources

picnic baskets, hampers
food and drink (real or
pretend)
plastic bottles for drinks
picnic plates and cups
plastic cutlery
tablecloth or blanket
a map
an umbrella for the rain
binoculars
camera

Vocabulary

journey
walk
grass/sand
choose
best place
sit down
food words (eg. drink/
sandwich)
share
view
watch
sunny/cloud/rain/
shelter
fly, wasp or bee

Literacy links

stories about picnics
lists
directions

Maths links

direction and position
time

Resources

bikes and trikes
notices on posts
clip board
money and till
price list
timer or clock
tickets
hat or uniform for person in
charge

Vocabulary

wait
turn
ticket
price
money/pay
back
finish
time is up
how long?
queue

Literacy links

travelling stories
bike books, magazines and
catalogues
lists

Maths links

money
time

Resources

play mat or other farm base
(in the summer use the
grass or draw a farm on the
ground)
animals
farm vehicles
sacks and bales
farm buildings, fences and
gates
small world people
signs

Vocabulary

animal names and
noises
adult and baby names
animal families
grow
harvest/cut
plough
collect
market
sell
count
field
escape

Literacy links

farm books and stories
lists and labels
maps and plans

Maths links

counting and sorting

Picnics
(outside or inside)

Domestic

Let's go on a picnic!

Fill a basket with food and drink, offer a tablecloth and they will be off!

Indoor picnics are just as much fun.

Bike hire
(outside)

Transactional

Hire a bike (or scooter, trike, pram or other big toy).

It will give practice with money and taking turns.

Farm
(small world)

Imagined places

Use the farm animals on a cement mixing tray, a farm mat or carpet tiles.

Introducing tractors, trucks and people as well as animals will make more fun.

Resources

use screens or large
sheets of card to make
a round house
cut out windows or make
with sea 'views'
a light on the roof
usual crockery, etc.
books and magazines
about boats and the sea
a boat outside to 'row'
fishing rods
rainproof clothes and
wellies

Vocabulary

light
shipwreck
rocks
boat
danger
home/homesick
land/sea
night
rescue
rope
helicopter
lifeboat
storm

Literacy links

lighthouse and sea
stories
letters

Maths links

time

Resources

sand or water tray (prop it
up a bit so the water runs
to one end)
sand
shells
play people
boats
deckchairs, etc.

Vocabulary

holiday
seaside
swim
deep
float
paddle
sit/sun/deckchair
shade
ice cream

Literacy links

seaside stories and
books
postcards from holiday
lists for packing
holiday clothes, food

Maths links

counting and sorting

Resources

this needs to be big and is
good outside (use a
climbing frame as a base if
you have one)
bandanas
curtain rings on elastic for
earrings
telescopes from cardboard
tubes
stripey jumpers
pirate hats
maps and treasure to find
pirate flag

Vocabulary

pirate
sail
boat
captain
capture
treasure
telescope

Literacy links

pirate stories and songs
notices

Maths links

distance
position

Lighthouse

Domestic

Living in a lighthouse is a new experience with many familiar features.

Lighthouse keepers need food, beds, furniture, just like those who live on land. A good way to explore similarities and differences.

An island
(small world in a sand or water tray)

Transactional

Use a sand or water tray to make a seaside.

Put some rocks in the water and even some boats to sail in.

Pirate ship

Imagined places

A pirate ship can be made from boxes, big bricks or crates.

Some costumes, curtain rings for earrings, a telescope and a flag for the top of the mast, then 'Sail Away!'

Resources

a screen covered in card with a wheel painted on the outside will work

a picture window with a 'view' of the country or seaside

seats that make into beds

water carriers

picnic table and chairs

sleeping bags

holiday brochures

camera

Vocabulary

stay
holiday
room
fold
tidy
careful
pack up
shopping
picnic
trip
playground
pay
booking

Literacy links

holiday brochures
stories about holidays and travellers
life in small spaces (eg. barges, tents)
lists for packing
holiday clothes
weather

Maths links

size and shape

Resources

outdoor wheeled toys

till and money

price labels

shopkeeper overalls or badges

posters and notices

counter table

open/closed sign

catalogues and brochures

bike magazines

maps and routes

sale and special offer signs

Vocabulary

sell
buy
price
two wheeled
three wheeled
saddle
size/measure
fit
try
surprise
colour
special offer
catalogue

Literacy links

make your own catalogue with photos of your toys or catalogue pictures
transport stories
lists
labels and diagrams

Maths links

money

Resources

playground chalk for roundabouts, crossroads and crossings

signs and notices

traffic lights

crossing signs

parking bays

garage and pumps

car wash

police uniforms

road worker stuff and cones

parking/crossing warden

phone box

Vocabulary

crossing
park
No Parking
careful
Green cross Code
safe/dangerous
drive
pedestrian
petrol
crossing

Literacy links

car and traffic stories
road safety
notices and signs
parking tickets

Maths links

money
position

Caravan

Domestic

Make a caravan outline with a big sheet of card and attach it to your home corner to make a new setting.

Fold away beds and a house on wheels will be a lot of fun.

Car and bike showroom

Transactional

Use outdoor toys to make a shop or showroom.

Let customers try the vehicles out before they buy them.

Make brochures and posters to advertise the toys, and have forms to fill in for the sale.

Driving

petrol, repairs, road safety (outside)

Imagined places

With the children, make a roadway with paint or chalk on the outside play area.

Don't forget pedestrian crossings, lights, crossroads and roundabouts.

Resources

bus drivers need the same things as every one else, but they may be on shifts and they will need somewhere to store their uniforms and make their sandwiches.

uniforms

several beds

'keep quiet' notices

sandwich boxes and equipment

food and drinks

Vocabulary

sleep
shift
disturb
today
tomorrow
time
packed lunch
tickets

Literacy links

stories about jobs and occupations
timetables
sequences of time and activities

Maths links

time
sequences

Resources

chairs in two rows
conductor's hat and bag
driver's hat/uniform
tickets and money
purses or bags for passengers
bus stops on stands
road markings
bus timetable
notice for bus to say where it is going (shops, school, garden centre, TV Land, etc.)

Vocabulary

ticket
bus
driver
conductor
pay
return
single
special
half fare
destination
stop
seat
stand

Literacy links

journeys and travel
books
timetables and notices
sequences

Maths links

money
direction
ordinal numbers

Resources

a big box with a TV screen cut out
cameras
dressing up for pop singers, DJs, announcers, sports people, travellers, wildlife experts, news readers
microphones
headphones
tape recorders
video cameras
DVD player

Vocabulary

camera
film
video
record
programme
announcer
news
favourite
smile
script

Literacy links

DVDs/videos of TV programmes to look at and talk about
fact books
TV magazines

Maths links

time

The bus driver's house

Domestic

Make your home area into a house for a family of bus drivers.

What sort of house would they live in?

A bus

Transactional

Arrange some chairs to make a bus inside or outside.

Don't forget some bus stops!

TV Land

Imagined places

Go to TV land and find out what it is like the other side of the TV screen!

You could be a cartoon character, a pop star or a famous person.

You could read the news, the weather or be a DJ.

Ideas for equipment and resources

▶ Concrete mixing trays from garden centres make good trays for small world play.

▶ Use dry pasta for 'cooking' in domestic play.

▶ Florists and charity shops are good sources for fake flowers.

▶ Florists will know where to get fake grass and flowers. They also often keep offcuts of florist's ribbon.

▶ White plastic sheeting can be used for road mats. Mix white glue with paint to make it stick on plastic for maps, hangings and cardboard to make structures.

▶ Try your local kitchen equipment shop for large cardboard boxes to make TVs, computers, washing machines. A washing machine box will make a house, or at least a wardrobe.

▶ For mirrors try plastic mirror tiles or stick-on mirror sheet. Toy departments sometimes have plastic mirrors with wiggly surfaces.

▶ Visit charity shops (Help the Aged, Oxfam, etc.) for kitchen items, men's clothes, baskets and bags, ornaments.

▶ Ask at your local vet and doctor for posters and leaflets (RSPCA, PDSA, Health Education Centres may also be able to help).

▶ Ask colleagues and parents to help you save junk mail for domestic play.

▶ Use old school equipment and mail order catalogues for labels and to make your own catalogues for role play.

▶ If you have access to a sewing machine, use it with no thread in to 'sew' sheets of paper in squares to make tear off stamps.

▶ Collect brochures from travel agents.

▶ Buy or beg hobby and interest magazines (eg. cycling, caravans, camping, wedding, etc.) to suit the focus of your current role play setting.

▶ A child's satchel makes a great postman's bag.

- Big tubes from inside carpet rolls make post boxes, pillars and signs. Use a saw to cut them and glue them to a wooden base with white glue. Smaller tubes are available from fabric shops.

- Ask your local shoe shop for some shoe boxes.

- Carpet samples are often thrown away when new ranges come in. Call at a few carpet shops and see what you can scrounge for role play.

- Ask colleagues to recycle envelopes (eg. from a school office).

- Ask a school kitchen or a cafe to keep big cans and buckets from catering.

- Buy paper bags for shops and plastic cutlery in bulk from a cash and carry.

- Net curtains and saris make wonderful veils and trains for brides.

- Try printing your own curtains and tablecloths with fruit or vegetables on old sheeting. See 'The Little Book of Science through Art' for techniques and equipment.

- Recycle packaging from fruit, cake and other food for shops and make food to fit.

- Buy garden sticks, plastic pots, seed and pot trays and growbags from garden centres to make your own centre.

- Cheap toyshop rings and necklaces will make any shop or wedding special. Make a trip to an Asian shop for some additional sparkle.

- You can get hats and wigs from educational suppliers, charity shops and rummage sales. (Don't forget to wash second hand ones or put them in the microwave to ensure they are free from inhabitants!)

- Use curtain rings for pirate earrings by threading them on elastic to fit around the ears.

- Get some broom handles and set them in buckets or tins of concrete or plaster to make stable posts for signs, notices and directions.

- A rope strung between two posts, trees or from fence to fence will make a hideout or tent if you drape a blanket or curtain over it. Use single bricks to hold the edges down.

- ▶ Screw a wooden batten to a wall or fence to make a secure and permanent place to pin notices and posters.

- ▶ Garden centres now sell reasonably priced gazebos and parasols to provide shade for outside activities, including role play.

- ▶ Look in educational catalogues for pop-up tents. They make good bases for imaginative play, and now come with connecting tunnels and other additional features.

- ▶ Make some petrol pumps with large cardboard tubes or tall boxes and a piece of hose from a DIY shop.

- ▶ Guttering and drainpipes make super roads, water ways and tunnels.

Make some simple dressing up tabards with minimal sewing

You need pieces of fabric about 1.5 metres long and about 50cm wide. Manmade fabrics are best because they don't crease, and crimplene type fabrics are the very best because they don't even need hemming!

1. Fold the fabric in half lengthways:

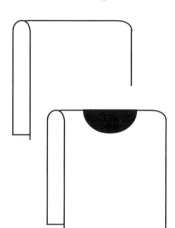

2. Cut out a neck hole (make sure it is big enough). If you use pinking shears, material is less likely to fray.

3. On the wrong side, paint a line of glue round the neckline to stop fraying (rubber solution such as Copydex works best).

4. Round the corners, put bits of Velcro on the sides to fasten, fringe the hems or hem the neck and edges if you like (the tabards will be fine if you haven't got time to do this). You might want to make a supply of these so they are ready when you need a ticket collector, shopkeeper or bus driver in a hurry!

5. Now you can write a title, paint a slogan or stick a picture on the front to make different characters.

Making food

Make food for your 'house' using these recipes. Paint the food when once it is baked, using a mixture of paint and white glue.

1. Uncooked dough

Mix
2 cups flour
1 cup salt
1 tablespoon oil
1 cup water.

Knead till smooth.

2. Cooked dough

In a pan, mix
1 cup flour
1 cup salt
4 teaspoons cream of tartar
2 tablespoons oil
2 cups water

Cook for 3 to 5 minutes, stirring until stiff.
Cool before use.
Store in a bag in the fridge.

Use either sort of dough to make fruit, vegetables, other foods, objects to sell. Bake in a slow oven for at least an hour, until the objects are hard right through.

Cool, then paint with a mixture of paint and white glue (this makes them shiny and more resistant to dropping!).